Impossible Lessons

Impossible Lessons

Jennifer Bullis

MoonPath Press

Copyright © 2013 Jennifer Bullis
all rights reserved

Poetry
ISBN 978-1-936657-07-0

Cover photo and author photo by Mark Kummer

Design by Tonya Namura
using Minion Pro

MoonPath Press is dedicated to publishing the
best poets of the U.S. Northwest Pacific states

MoonPath Press
PO Box 1808
Kingston, WA 98346

MoonPathPress@yahoo.com

http://MoonPathPress.com

To my husband, Mark Kummer, and
our son, John Benjamin

Acknowledgements

Grateful acknowledgement is made to the editors of the following journals and anthologies, in which these poems, some in slightly different versions, first appeared:

Avocet: A Journal of Nature Poems: "A Dream, a Bird"

Cascadia Review: "Day After Thanksgiving," "One Way," "Strange Bird," and "Went Hiking"

Clover: A Literary Rag: "Thus the World"

The Comstock Review: "Basal Cell Carcinoma"

Crosscurrents: Journal of the Washington Community College Humanities Association: "Ascent," "Climate Change," and "Lesson Horse"

Crux: "Hide and Seek"

Floating Bridge Review: "Lesson Horse," "My Neighbor," and "Start What You Finish"

Iron Horse Literary Review: "Some Friend"

Pontoon: An Anthology of Washington State Poets: "Ascent" and "Body, Blood"

Rock & Sling: "Strange Accounting"

Sqajet: "What Is Nature?"

Umbrella: "Placebo Effect" and "For J.B., in the Sixth Month"

Gratitude

I deeply appreciate the generous words, mentoring, and encouragement of Louise Bullis, Jeffrey Klausman, Sherri Winans, Luci Shaw, Mark Jarman, Scott Dalgarno, John Shaw, Marya Smith, Carol Lichtenberg, Scott Cairns, James Bertolino, J. I. Kleinberg, Jeanne Yeasting, Anita K. Boyle, Jeremy Voigt, and Andrew Shattuck McBride, with special gratitude to Andrew for his suggestions on this manuscript. I also thank Whatcom Community College for two quarters of sabbatical leave during which several of these poems were written. And my sincere appreciation to Lana Hechtman Ayers, for choosing my work, for her warmth and generosity, and for her artful editing of this volume.

Contents

I

Start What You Finish	5
Grandmother, Rasping	6
Climate Change	7
Basal Cell Carcinoma	9
Ten Great Gifts for the Woman Who Has Nothing	11
Eve Reflects	12
Mary Speaks from Her Wooden Crèche	13
For Lent	14
For J.B., in the Sixth Month	15
Among Swallows and Horses, Working Out My Post-Critical Subjecthood	16

II

Cover Letter from the Goddess	21
The Ancient Women Reply	22
To Wallace Stevens, of Hartford and Key West	23
Awaiting the Muse	24
What Is Nature?	25
Test Kitchen	26
Walking Wolf Creek Road, Methow Valley, October	27
Crossing the Methow at the Tawlks-Foster Suspension Bridge	29

Hide and Seek	30
A Dream, a Bird	31
Strange Bird	32

III

Some Friend	35
Placebo Effect	37
Infusion at Starbucks	38
Greetings to the New Poet	39
The Answer	41
Lesson Horse	42

IV

My Neighbor	47
Thus the World	49
Strange Accounting	50
Ascent	51
Went Hiking	52
Day After Thanksgiving	53
Body, Blood	54
One Way	55
Notes on the Epigraphs	57
About the Author	58

Impossible Lessons

I

Start What You Finish

Cooking, Mother prayed and sang
while the gods fashioned me
under her voice. The gazelle on Mother's fire

fed me back to the gods. Over supper
Father said, We'll call the baby Umbra,
or Nimbus, or Manna. Under Mother's

feet, the gods fashioned gazelles
from our ancestors. Mother said,
Milk me, honey me, call me Sweetgoat.

Over her music, Father fashioned gods
from the grasslands. The gods sang,
Give us you, burn us you, we

are hungry.

Grandmother, Rasping

Grandmother, rasping
her thinnest bow-saw blade
through a fist-sized cantaloupe,
surgeoned apart its two salmon halves
and examined the seeds patterned there

in the shivering pulp.
If arrayed in veins, the seeds
presaged lifelong independence
for me; if they shaped a star,
I would be fated to marry.

If the pulp's quantum world
ripped randomly, Grandmother
would gently wrench the neck
of another small melon from
her garden, begin again

with her shaman's question.
Thus did she implant in me
lifelong dread. We grandkids
were the only family she ever kissed:
my brother, a cherished intrusion;

I, a figment of her being alone.

Climate Change

It's roses already, this hot May,
usually the month of rhododendrons'
and buttercups' blooming—but this year
the lilacs have finished early,
like the tulips before them, and now
it's the roses pried open by the early heat.
The bees rush around loading their legs
with pollen they know won't last:

spring and summer compressed
hold a meaning too urgent
to waste time pondering it.
I dreamed last night
of visiting my grandmother,
also a Rose, and of her not hearing
my knock and call at her door.
I had emeralds for her, in a box held

in my two flat palms, and I watched
through the glass front door
as she moved about in her living room.
Unsurprised at her nakedness,
I noticed instead the flesh she had put on—
her frail frame of nine decades
suddenly rounded and robust.
Not gone backward in time,

into her younger body, but forward,
so that her curvaceous form moved
with anticipation, now, as she continued

not to hear me knocking, deaf
to all but her own faint humming,
humming in the middle days of spring
as she loaded living
onto her legs.

Basal Cell Carcinoma

The doctor tells me it has become
locally invasive, it must come off, it will leave
a leaf-shaped scar along my collarbone.
I drive home dreading the knife next week
despite his assurances that the excision

will only sting, that I am in little danger
so long as I watch for further growths.
At home, you are making one of your
new recipes from the Santa Fe gourmet
school. You chop three kinds of chiles

and explain to me their three kinds of heat.
Listening, I can think of only *sear* and *slice*.
Then you tell me about the other ingredient,
basil, how it will contrast the chiles. Basil
brightens the other flavors, basil contributes

tang, basil cools the palate, calms the throat,
you tell me. Each time you repeat the word
I hear *basal, basal*, spelling it after cancer
in the dictionary of my ear. At first annoyed
that you are talking food in the face of this

tumor consuming my skin, I begin, as you
go on, to sense the wisdom of making supper
instead of hosting a panic in honor of my
alarm. You pull basil stems from the vase
by the sink, rinse them, sever the leaves

from their stalks, slice them lengthwise
on a pale board. I breathe their scent, a cold
fragrance, and begin to believe that dread
might be merely a smell, or fear just a leaf
I can eat for the tang, for the sting.

Ten Great Gifts for the Woman Who Has Nothing

For the journey out, figs.

Fig leaves
for carrying the blame.

A womb, and a man
worthy to name it.

Another rib and even more backbone.

The pomegranate, secrets still intact.

Anklet of snakeskin, woven bracelet of grass.

A circlet of worry
for her newly conscious brow,

for her hair still smelling
of blossoms and smoke.

Eve Reflects

From time to time my bite is a waking
to the lift of thought, to the press
of deciding. Occasionally my taste

is a meteor bolting from the windowed
castle of the moon into the slim shadow
of my turning.

At times that apricot is all I know
of the globe, a blushing tear
I net with the small hairs on my cheek.

Now and then my swallowing
is a long drop out of cloudy agreement
into firm thought. From time

to time my temptation is a dance step
named curiosity, a low bounce with a glance
into wondering. Now and again

my teeth are a near miss,
depending on the compass of the reader
who is turning to the page

where I am being made. Every so often
the weight of my soul is suspended
in that lamplight.

From time to time all my words fit
on a single petal, small and pitted—
a bruised gift I cup in my hand.

Mary Speaks from Her Wooden Crèche

Here comes the wobbling toddler.
Today he swats at the roof's thatched straw
and clumsily fingers the carved sheep,

knocks down Joseph and the two taller Magi,
and selects the head of one gray ox
for gnawing. I, the mother bewildered

and blue, keep staring at my lean wooden baby,
whose own beatific eyes stare at the live child
at his feet. The toddler plucks a donkey

from the straw, mouths it, drops it
to the floor in a splash of drool, goes back
to teething on the ox. I pray that lowly molar

one day will be exalted. May both left hand
and right gain in dexterity. May the milled
skeletons of trees sprout green buds. May

the blood's gush across every altar cease
at the decree of some deity of reversals.
Now the toddler holds up two fingers,

as if in benediction, to the cradled figure
of my infant, who watches him reaching
and greedily grasping, and lets him.

For Lent

Pregnant, nauseous, I can only fast,
feeding the little creature whatever my flesh

and bones have to offer—protein, calcium—
and of my blood, the water s/he needs.

In this, my first ritual observance,
I can eat and drink only poetry, words solid

and liquid passing through my eyes,
nourishing a soul as hungry as my body.

I am losing weight, two pounds a week
from my small frame, but putting on

images, a bulk of them growing
in the belly of my mind, swelling

in murk and fluid and bringing
some words, if blessed, to bear.

For J.B., in the Sixth Month

> *[I]n their terminal structure, narrations are rehearsals for death...*
> —George Steiner

This, then, will be no narration. You I am
gestating toward breath, and your heart
arrhythmia notwithstanding, I withstand

the knowledge that its beats are, ultimately,
finite. Sure, death is the other that waits
for us both, but you are the other other

I encounter in the strange labyrinths of my
own tissue. Under my heart and its slower
pulsing, you hear me speak and sing. Later,

altered, you will claim language for yourself
when you perceive that I am other than
you. Will you recall enough, then, to tell me

the story of the marching band we hear now
rehearsing on the lawn under my office window?
Their drumbeat irresistible, I rock, I rock

you, side to side in my chair. Confined
to their tiny square of grass, the musicians
cannot march, so they are dancing.

Among Swallows and Horses, Working Out My Post-Critical Subjecthood

The swallows swivel and bank, out and back
in, while I muck the horse stalls.
No longer emblems of Procne or Philomela,

the swallows signal only that the bugs have hatched,
that they've returned to catch them, sixty
mosquitoes and flies per hour each,

to feed to their hatchlings. All eyes and beaks,
the cup-nested young perch in the barn rafters,
and between their noisy feedings

watch me interrogate my good luck
to be working among horses and the soft bodies
of birds. Is it wrong to want to say that they mean

something other than their otherness from me?
In ancient times, the stories linked
humans to every conceivable type of wing.

A professor taught me that mythmaking
is the verbal construction of hegemony
over the unknowable. This was one way in which

going to graduate school was like taking
your inner child to be circumcised: first
the liturgy, then sharpness, and shrieking.

But keeping covenant carries risk
in exchange for new ways of getting
your questions answered. And still,

theories drift down to me like small feathers
while I rake and shovel below the nests—like blessings,
soft, even to a girl bereft of her tongue.

II

II

Cover Letter from the Goddess

Dear Prospective Employer:

After some two millennia away
to raise my sons, I seek to re-enter
the workforce of the paid. To your team, I bring
sheaves of wheat and solar panels, as well
as new remedies for your seasonal allergies.

I produce at the rate of one new king
every fourth winter and a new crop
of candidates every fourth spring.
If you are a locavore, I can grow
an entire village for you to eat.

I can stem your flood of customer complaints
and bloom wherever you choose to plant the pieces
of my brother. I have a strong record
of making ends meet beginnings
and holding it all together on a shoestring.

For compensation, I expect
an executive range. Three to thirteen
members in upper management
annually should meet my needs.

I invite you to a luncheon interview
on Aventine Hill at your convenience.
Please bring wine, oil, and a white bull calf,
and my slim assistants will greet you from the trees.

The Ancient Women Reply

*The worlds revolve like ancient women
Gathering fuel in vacant lots.*
—T.S. Eliot

We *are* those revolving worlds. Your words
call us into being—we who have been here
all along. We were the mermaids,
we did sing for you, we were the rescuers
of your scuttled crustacean claw,
the globed peaches of your highest daring.

While you stir coffee-spoonfuls of your melancholy
into the smoke and brine of the era and peer at us
through your streaked, distancing spectacles,
hear: we did make the world go round, still do.
We will you to go on being moved
by your curling fancies in this living, blackened land,
and sing, keep singing, of the suffering
and the gentleness that do not end.

To Wallace Stevens, of Hartford and Key West

The palm at the end of the mind,
Beyond the last thought, rises
In the bronze decor...

Dear Sir:

Even your difficulty endures.
Your system of symbols—green,
for instance, the color of truth—
is obscure, formidable.

And then, you found the truth
too lush a tropic, as verdant
and venereal as Florida, disclosing
too many things even to her lover,

muddling your actuarial mind.
A rage for order fanned your ship
back north: a climate better suited
to your intellect, wintry and exact.

What is clear is that despite your
stated farewell, your imagination
never quite got free of her.
A few things for themselves persisted:

a fascination with the shimmering deep,
a horizon beyond any tidy idea, beckoning
to you greenly like a waving palm
at the other end of the mind.

Awaiting the Muse

The wind has changed direction
and from land, the bay
looks angry about something.

Listen: the wind is imposing secrets
on the whitecaps. The cedars hum
and the maple leaves crack.

Try, and you can see the firs
arrowing up from the little island
inhabited only by ancestors.

This north wind dries and tugs
like a local moon forbidding stasis,
like the fact of the ocean, there always

with its lifting and pulling down,
its constant sounds, its vastness,
a source and a cold threat.

What buoyant thing can save me?
What offers warmth but the small songs
invented from my fear?

What Is Nature?

October, Guemes Island

It's wild roses, the tangled ones,
with thorns, overgrowing the old cattle farm
where the artist who bought it cared five years
for his failing mother. Or a space
newly cleared in the cedars and firs for the new
house, with no footpath from the old
across acres of pasture grown dense
with alder saplings at the edge of the woods.
And the echoes of fattened Herefords crossing
Guemes Channel by ferry to the slaughterhouse
in Stanwood. Or a man's long kindnesses
to the woman who gave him
himself. And a house you can't walk to
from here, a reality mediated by trees,
by all the reasons we seek them.
Or October, a sparrow hovering,
the rose hips on the bare vines, reddening.

Test Kitchen

With what threat will I next endanger the sky?
Just walking toward the sink brings on another spark.

I begin making coffee, lift my eyes to the window—
two molting crows play with a drifting feather.

Their flight maps a draping grid
across the thunderclouds.

How do you funnel all your intentions
into a one-teaspoon poem?

The trick is to take it all in. The trick
is to be single-minded.

Already I have said nothing.
How much more of this can I forgive?

I make twenty or thirty of these mistakes
just trying to fix breakfast.

Please wash up and sit down. Please
dish your crackling allegory right here.

Let's pretend the char doesn't bother us.
Let's pretend this smoke won't happen again.

Walking Wolf Creek Road, Methow Valley, October

After I cross the creek
in the meadow, the wind
wraps itself around my shoulders

like a cold shawl and draws me
toward the woods.
There, fir and Ponderosa

space my breaths between gusts.
I'm certain I can read
what the dry grasses write

on the air with their slender
quills: that my steps take care
not to erase the prints

of the deer that inscribed
its delicate passage on this trail
just since this morning's rain.

Where is this deer going,
with its own walking steps
and springy trotting strides?

I hope I will find it near the river
to greet and to tell: I have known
all along what it meant

in pressing its feet over and over
into the damp soil of the earth,
have understood fully the joyful intent

propelling the body among pines
and the scribbling grasses
and the cloaking wind.

Crossing the Methow at the Tawlks-Foster Suspension Bridge

After William Stafford's "Where We Are"

Daylight loves everything coming up this river
like the fog, like the slow reveal
of a poet's seeing as he stands

on this swaying bridge suspended
over the swift channel of his imagining.
Walking this footpath so many years

behind him, I stand atop the bridge's curve
and look downriver, the sun setting behind me
loving the wet sky violet.

An oxbow moon floats on the horizon
as gold cottonwoods shuffle their starlings
from one branch to another

and finally breathe them out over the river's
mottled glow. Every bird's flight
renews my eyes' slow marveling,

like the rain locating boulders under its feet,
friendly, stepping and tapping
and greeting them one at a time.

Hide and Seek

All flesh is grass...
      —Isaiah 40:6

For a moment, I find you
hiding yourself in yourself
as grass hides itself in a meadow,

blade behind blade behind stem,
or as leaves conceal themselves
in forests. You extend yourself

into the particulars of matter:
into blood cells, plant fibers,
grains of granite, the rays

that fire chlorophyll.
From beyond our universe,
you hold all its spinnings—

yet sprout within it,
cut down and living,
God in the grass.

A Dream, a Bird

A profusion of blue feathers,
turquoise and violet, cerulean.
Like a peacock in its spectrum

but profounder in its knowing—
an eagle, perhaps, or an iridescent
raven. It was a messenger
and a message,

the wording of which I cannot remember,
but the substance sensed,
with me and in me like breath
ruffled by wings.

And the intensity of its presence
like the gift of seeing a hummingbird close by,
its thrum hovering over blossoms—

and after it buzzes upward and recedes,
glinting, back into the sky,
the fullness of the silence.

Strange Bird

What bird are you? Hawk-shaped, gray,
tail striped and neck ringed in white,
you hover and swoop, low, a few feet above
the hay stubble, spying for mice.

Once, you dart down,
scramble in the grass, lost to my view
as you sate your raptor's appetite on some
ground-bound creature.

But if hunting's your purpose, why
do you round me in your orbits,
line me in your sights, between flights
to the field's far corners? What am I to you?

I wonder further, amble the field—
then you return again, hover,
and drop this poem
into my mouth.

III

Some Friend

Towards Helen I am peeved.
She refuses to participate in my mythopoeisis.
She told me, *Honey, last time you took up*
that project, your wings went all waxy.
True, but someone was roasting an ibex
and I couldn't be bothered. The fact is,
she doesn't approve of the way my three
breasts line up. She says I'd need
nine heads and two more guitars
even to begin to pull off the cubist effect.
Can a girl just get a little veneration?
When we were kids, Helen flat refused
to play loom-and-spindle with me even when
I said she could be Weaverwoman of the Universe.
She still gets snide when I embroider any yarn.
She dislikes my searching for the fragments of Osiris
and re-membering his torn body. But
the last straw seemed to be when I pleaded
her to bridesmaid my next wedding to a new
Druid king. See, as priestess-queen,
at the end of his short reign,
I sacrifice him to ensure good harvest.
Helen snorted, *Girlfriend, there is no way*
in God's green erogenous zone I will
tart up so you can knock off another monarch
in his prime. I begged, *But the old symbols!*
They're falling away! Please, won't you just
re-enact with a sipped cup even one
of the old-time rituals? Helen replied
with a stop-hand and a shake-head saying,

Lovegirl, I'm not that into you.
But all I want is reverence where
reverence is due.

Placebo Effect

So I go to the doctor of philosophy
for my annual metaphysical. He asks me
the usual questions: *Any irregularity
with your epistemology? Are the meds
still helping with those intermittent bouts
of doubt?* I tell him, *Yes, but recently
they have taken on a hyper-Cartesian tinge,
going beyond the use of "not"
as a helpful tool for testing a suspect reality.
The problem has progressed to a troublesome
tendency toward generalized negation,
a habit of rejecting every supposition.*
The doc says, *Then we'd better increase
your dosage to get this under control.
With your phenomenological pressure
so elevated, I think you are at risk of rupture.*
Well, I say, *that may be, but how would you know?*
He's good, that doc. He comes right back with,
How do you know that you're not?
So we agree I'll try a higher dose.
But don't go thinking I am going to believe
that it will work.

Infusion at Starbucks

It is the oldest war
where moose becomes wolf and crow
...
where we are still afraid.
             —Linda Hogan

Reading, sipping, I picture the food chain
as the membrane linking fear with ancestry—
the living tissue joining our terror of death
to the apparent endlessness (given our history
of begetting and eating) of life and blood

flooding the earth. Some are broken open
that others may live; the others are broken
likewise, later. But who profits from, say,
malady? I pose the question to the mermaid logo
displayed like the icon of a deity high up

on the red wall of the coffeehouse. Two women
about my age at the adjacent table speak praise
of their kind oncologist, who has asked them
what music they would like to soothe them
during chemo, what flavor of stomach buffer

they prefer. I imagine the only choice
must be blood, the sole solution infusing their veins
or mine, the sustenance gained from the body
of an abstract other, lending one generation hope
for a little-longer life.

Greetings to the New Poet

1. Socrates to the New Poet

Congratulations. You have discovered the oneness
of The Good, The True, and The Beautiful.
Though I bar you from governing, I commend you
for being in love.

2. The Buddha to the New Poet

The good is illusory, the true is mutable,
the beautiful is in the eye
of the impermanent.
Have compassion on them, for they
shall see death.

3. Wallace Stevens to the New Poet

Death is the mother of beauty, else I am
no modernist. Congratulations
on your discovery that writing poems
is a means of rubbing up against
the gold, indifferent shins of the divine.

4. Jesus to the New Poet

I say unto you, death is no more
than the mother of beauty.
And the kingdom of Heaven is like

my thousand secret names
dropping onto your tongue
unbidden. In this world
of becoming, I am the first draft,
the final revision, all
that you have been looking for.
Go in peace.

5. Philip Larkin to the New Poet

They fuck you up, these imposing voices
of the fathers. Anyhow, congratulations:
you have succumbed to the allure
of the good and the true. Beautiful,
that you have given me the last word.
Go, and sin no more.

The Answer

After the windstorm, a pileated woodpecker
works the dead trunk of a newly leaning maple.

He pulls his scarlet-crested head back
the full length of his black and white body

with each pounding stroke of his beak,
scattering moss, bark, bits of rotted wood

on the forest floor. I want to know
why his head is shaped like an anvil

and why he is fated to hammer
for his food. I want to know why

this particular maple snag has lost its footing
among so many of its neighbors.

I crave a sound rationale as to how
this one, of all of them, was singled out

by the beetles and fungi that killed it
in the first place. But I learn nothing

except by the woodpecker's breaking off
his analysis of the tree and flashing past

all my questioning, the red crest of his head
a sweet and vivid and impossible lesson.

Lesson Horse

I trailer you home from the stable
where I have left you while I was away
for the summer. You are gaunt,

hollow-eyed, a dispirited rack of bones
under faded orange hide. The barn manager
had promised me you'd be exercised as a

lesson horse, and indeed you have taught me
never to entrust to another the work
my own heart hands me.

I settle you into your stall at home
and arrange the pasture fences so as
to manage your hunger:

one full day's grazing on sweet grass
would sicken you worse than three months'
underfeeding. I give you instead

many small handfuls of alfalfa hay,
the proteinous stalks crumbling richly
in your teeth. Hand-feeding you is solace

against the tear inside my chest, like fulfillment
of a late assignment, or hope
storing up in your thin tissues for the day

when I can exercise you myself again,
and you turn leaf and stem and longing
into muscle. The one strength

you haven't lost is your robust forgiving
of everything past, your attention now
on the food in front of you, my open hand.

ID_NOT_FOUND

IV

My Neighbor

So much depends
upon the weather.
If the next wave
of the storm holds off,
then the only perils
likely to threaten
these three loose roosters,
self-assured but naïve
and pecking for food
in my garden beside
the rusting horse trailer,
will be roaming dogs
and the traffic. But if,
as predicted, the wind
kicks up, the high gusts
will tumble these tame birds
straight across the road
and into the deep ditch
swollen with rain
water.

Last time I spoke with
the neighbor who owns them
was to squabble over payment
for paving our shared access
road (my property, his use).
After I agreed
to split the cost fifty-
fifty, he didn't even
repair my pasture fence

when the contractor's truck
backed into a post. I suppose
I should have suggested
we mend it together, but
even though I have read
that poem, too, I didn't feel
much like talking.

Yet I decide
to crate up the roosters
and haul them next door
where they belong.
As I push them in my red
wheelbarrow up the long,
smooth driveway,
the wind picks up,
and the clouds glazing the sky
release their rain water, hard
and gray like stones.

Thus the World

> *[T]hus the world is full of leaves and feathers,*
> *and comfort, and instruction.*
> —Mary Oliver

Over the grave of the old horse
gone one year, goldfinches—
dozens, hovering,

feasting on seeds of thistles
flourishing in the soil disturbed
by the backhoe.

Into the air the birds cast their trills,
their bright yellow, a little
comfort.

Strange Accounting

Grieving Tomcat, flattened in the road
Easter morning, I told over the litany
of his many names and nicknames
and wept, harder, at "Daffodil." His orange
tabby patches and white roundnesses,
the blameless pink of his nose and mouth
and ears, had all suggested increase

of blooming and brightness. Amid the lilies,
I always forget: this is my season of loss,
of wondering what to do with loss, of watching
as the cosmic accounts are reconciled
by means of a heroic and terrible dying.
I struggle to understand this system of bookkeeping.
Still, the ultimate audit intrigues me,

and that night I re-read the Franciscan
who says that when you are resurrected, all
that your heart has loved is resurrected with you.
And so I prayed for salvation, not so much
for my own body as for the eventual unburying
of fur, of purr and pink and scamper,
and the everness of springtime without passing.

Ascent

> *The natural property of a wing is to raise that which is heavy and carry it aloft to the region where the gods dwell.*
> —Socrates

True. But what of this whiskey-jack
presently harrying me to hand over my snack
of chocolate-covered espresso beans? I regret, Socrates,
that I am having trouble glimpsing transcendence

in this gray, uncrested jay's brazen flappings
at my face. Sorry, lovely bird, but I am
clean out of trail mix, and these caffeine beans
would burst your lovely bird heart.

Consider instead that we, both of us on this
Cascade summit, are a little elevated already.
Even if we have not yet ascended to the dwelling place
of the gods, at least we have made it

to the region of the huckleberries
that they have provided for us. Direct your wings
toward those blue spheres, and you will carry aloft
that which in me is heavy from its racing.

Went Hiking

Up the river, as Annie Dillard
urged, to receive the revelations,
view the secrecies set aside

for the loving seeker.
Seeking salmon,
the fall run, said to be

swimming the river now
and up the steep tributaries.
Salmon struggling upstream

in search of mates
and annihilation. All
the waterways in flood

after hard rains, so muddy
that seeing in is impossible.
So, saw no salmon. No

eagles either. Not herons,
not otters, not coyotes.
But more alluring to the lover

is one secret well kept
than a thousand
easy confessions.

Day After Thanksgiving

This razor-bright morning, I hike the South Fork
of the Nooksack to see the salmon running.
Up from oceans, following some scent of granite,
they've sliced their way to these beds of gravel
to spawn and die. More are dead, now,
than swimming, in the water sharded at its edges
by ice, their brown and silver bodies piling
where the steep stream pools.

I hike higher, up a logging road, its skin graveled
with small stones like salmon scales
and layered with copper leaves:
fish-shaped, blade-like, their centers rotting,
serrated edges glinting and steely with frost.

I rest at the edge of a clear cut and watch
the peaks of the Twin Sisters tear
their slow bite into the sky—rock and snow
piercing the blue—and ponder how all this dying
puts a point on the tip of gratitude,
hooking in the throat like barb-cold air,
sharp like salt on the tongue.

Body, Blood

After Andrew Hudgins

So I'm standing over the sink de-boning a chicken
and feeling guilty, as always, at being about to eat
one of my fellow creatures, when I start hearing,
quiet-like, the name *Jesus, Jesus*, in every one of my ears
and then I realize the sound is talking at least partly

about the chicken, that it is holy, that in eating it
I will be receiving holiness into my body, too,
that my body is in fact already holy but thanks
to the holy chicken will be continuing alive, and that
the worrisome issue of the chicken having to die

is not actually so when I consider that it is Jesus,
that it is all Jesus (me, the chicken, the knife),
Jesus is constantly perishing onto our dinner tables
and reinventing himself as us, as more chickens, as
the whole boned and un-boned rest of the world.

One Way

I drive the one-way road around the lake,
listening to a radio piece about a species
of tiny fly, *ephemeroptera*,
that lives just one day before the failure
of its iridescent wings.

                      I begin my walk
and from the path above the lake
hear the *plook* of fish jumping for insects.
I turn every time to look, trying
to land my eye on the sound of the leap,
but never succeed in time to see more
than the ripples unfolding themselves
into the lake's smooth surface.

Back in my car, rounding the rest
of the road along the lake, I tune the radio
to a discussion of Andy Goldsworthy's art:
how he sculpts with ice, leaves,
twigs, how his chief medium is time.
How his pieces are products
as much of their own unmaking as of
his making them.

                      At dusk, a meteor
catches my vision by the periphery
and burns back into darkness
before I can pull it into focus.
But I see that its final flaring
is pink. That it's true, you never can
go home again. That some time soon
now, you will.

Notes on the Epigraphs

"For J.B., in the Sixth Month": from George Steiner, *Real Presences*. London: Faber and Faber, 1991 (141).

"The Ancient Women Reply": from T. S. Eliot, "Preludes" IV, in *T. S. Eliot: The Complete Poems and Plays 1909-1950*. Ed. Esme Valerie Eliot. New York: Harcourt, Brace & World, Inc., 1971 (13).

"To Wallace Stevens, of Hartford and Key West": from Wallace Stevens, "Of Mere Being," in *The Palm at the End of the Mind: Selected Poems and a Play*. Ed. Holly Stevens. New York: Vintage Books, 1971 (398).

"Infusion at Starbucks": from Linda Hogan, "Crow Law," in *The Book of Medicines: Poems*. Minneapolis: Coffee House Press, 1993 (31).

"Thus the World": from Mary Oliver, "The Dipper," in *Owls and Other Fantasies: Poems and Essays*. Boston: Beacon Press, 2003 (2-3).

"Ascent": from Plato, *The Phaedrus*, section 246e.

About the Author

Jennifer Bullis grew up in Reno, Nevada, and attended college and graduate school in California. While finishing a PhD in English at UC Davis, she and her husband, seeking a green place to live, moved to western Washington. She taught writing and literature at Whatcom Community College for fourteen years before sneaking away to write, hike, and chase after their son.

Her poems appear in journals and anthologies including *Iron Horse Literary Review*, *Natural Bridge*, *Conversations Across Borders*, *The Comstock Review*, *Floating Bridge Review/Pontoon*, *Cascadia Review*, *Clover*, and *Umbrella*. She won The Pitch contest at *Poetry Northwest* and received Honorable Mention in the Tupelo Press Poetry Project. She served on the Board of the Whatcom Poetry Series and blogs about "Poetry at the Intersection of Mythology and Hiking" at www.jenniferbullis.wordpress.com.

She lives in Bellingham with her family, which, by her current reckoning, includes a horse, two cats, and too many feathered, furry, and leafy creatures to count.

www.ingramcontent.com/pod-product-compliance
Lightning Source LLC
Chambersburg PA
CBHW031214090426
42736CB00009B/911